MARIA R. RIEGGER

Legal Issues Authors Must Consider

Eighth
House
Press

First published by Eighth House Press, LLC 2022

Copyright © 2022 by Maria R. Riegger

First edition

ISBN: 979-8-9863689-1-7

This book was professionally typeset on Reedsy.
Find out more at reedsy.com

To all my law school friends.

Contents

Foreword

First, nothing in this book constitutes legal advice.

Now that that disclaimer is out of the way, let's get down to it.

Authors ask all the time about the legal issues they need to think about when writing and publishing their books. They ask whether they should create a company to publish, and how to do that. They ask how to copyright their work and how to get permission to use copyrighted material. They ask whether they can write about real people without legal repercussions.

The purpose of this book is to address those questions around the areas of limited liability protection, copyright, and defamation. The information contained herein will help you protect yourself against potential liability. The steps and recommendations outlined below are fairly easy to take. Moreover, you can do them yourself.

You do not need an attorney to take the steps outlined in this book. That being said, it is good practice to consult with a local attorney if you are unsure about any legal issues and in order to know your rights. For example, you can certainly hire an attorney to set up a company for your author business, especially if you are overwhelmed with other things. It is always a good idea to delegate and subcontract work so that you can focus on writing.

Please beware of any legal and business-related advice you see online. There is a ton of inaccurate information and advice in online writing groups. People frequently respond to legal questions as if they know the answer. Usually, they are wrong. Most of the legal issues set forth in this guide depend on the law of the relevant state. As such, there is rarely a one-size-fits-all legal answer.

Since many of the issues in this guide are state-specific, the only way to know the precise answers to your questions is to either do the legal research yourself, or to consult with a local attorney in your jurisdiction. Moreover, a local attorney can also tell you the overall culture and climate of the judiciary in your jurisdiction, should you ever find yourself facing potential litigation. You cannot get all of that information in a one-size-fits-all soundbite or Facebook post.

Legal advice is certainly expensive. But the soundness of mind it brings you may well be worth the cost of a one-hour consultation. To be fair, in the United States the cost of a one-hour legal consultation varies greatly depending on your state and city or county. There are also free legal clinics from which you can seek legal advice, depending on your income level.

Writing and selling books is a business. Writing is, for myself included, largely a creative endeavor. However, we must understand that it is ultimately a profitable business. This guide is intended for those self-published authors who are interested in earning a living from writing and selling books.

If you only publish one book to see your name in print (which is perfectly fine if that's what you want), and do not plan to publish anything else or make any money from selling books, then many of the recommendations in this book will not be as useful to you. However, if you are interested in earning a profit from writing and selling books, and in setting up a business structure from which to do that, then this book is for you.

Lastly, the recommendations provided below are from a United States perspective. I live in the United States, and am licensed to practice law in the state of Virginia. I can therefore tell you the law in Virginia, but certainly cannot speak to the laws in every state.

Nevertheless, whatever jurisdiction or country you are located in, this information will help you by giving you a checklist from which to work, and a framework from which to build and protect your author business. Because your career as an author is just that. A business.

Limited Liability Protection

This section is all about why it is a good idea to set up a corporate entity to publish your books. This section provides you information on how to set up your business entity and sets the basis for the other legal issues addressed later in this guide.

First, you do not NEED to set up a business entity in order to run an author business. You can operate as a sole proprietor. However, while you do not need to set up a corporate entity, it is highly recommended that you do so. The biggest reason to operate your author business through a corporate entity can be summed up in two words: *limited liability.*

Establish a corporate entity to get limited liability protection

Many self-published authors publish under their own names. When you do so, the copyright page includes a line that looks like this: Legal Issues Authors Must Consider © 2022 by Maria R. Riegger.

When you publish under your own name, you are publishing as a sole proprietor, i.e., as an individual, not as a corporate entity.

The problem with publishing as a sole proprietor is that there is no legal division between you, the individual with your personal money and assets, and your author business. This means that if anyone were to sue you, ALL of your personal assets, including savings accounts, real estate, retirement accounts, etc., could potentially be awarded to the Plaintiff in a lawsuit. To most people, this would be terrifying.

If you are just starting out, newly published, you may think that it is unlikely that you would be sued for anything. You may also think that no one would bother to sue you because you are not making that much money in book sales.

First, people rarely *expect* to be sued. Unfortunately, many people are sued in frivolous lawsuits. It's stressful. Limiting your liability is good business practice and gives you peace of mind that your personal and family assets cannot be lost in a lawsuit.

Second, the idea that you do not make enough money from your author business is a scarcity, limited-belief mindset. I want you to have an abundance mindset. I want you to believe that you are going to publish multiple books, and that you are going to make a lot of money. I want you to think and act like a business-minded author. And I want you to make sure that your assets are protected.

To avoid this potential pitfall, it is highly recommended that you set up a corporate entity and publish your books under the entity name. Many people seem to think that setting up a corporate entity for their writing business is a big, scary thing. But it's really simple, and we'll go through it step-by-step.

First, I will talk about how to technically set up your limited liability entity. In doing so, I will focus on the limited liability company (LLC), the most popular entity for small businesses in the United States. I will also address the corporation. Next, I will talk about what you need to do to protect your personal assets and income and keep them separate from those of your business entity.

The limited liability company (LLC)

The LLC is the most popular corporate entity in the United States today. It is fairly simple to set up and maintain. The LLC is especially useful for small businesses, as it requires less paperwork and technical requirements than the corporation (discussed below). To this end, it is recommended that you set up an LLC through which you publish your books.

In the United States, the establishment and maintenance of LLCs and other corporate entities are regulated by the state governments. Each state has its own law that sets forth the rules and requirements to establish and operate an LLC. For example, Virginia has the Virginia Limited Liability Company Act. Therefore, any issues that arise regarding LLCs are typically governed by state laws, which obviously may differ. For this reason, it is advisable that you consult with a local attorney in your jurisdiction if you want help setting up the LLC and meeting the LLC requirements.

How to establish your LLC

To set up the LLC, you need to visit your state corporate commission website. In Virginia, go to https://www.scc.virginia.gov/ and click on *Create a New Business*. Make sure that you search the database of corporate entities for your business name to make sure that you do not use a name that already exists. This step is

3

important so that you are not challenged in court at a later date because you are using another company's name.

It is also recommended that you search the U.S. Patent and Trademark Office's federal trademark database to make sure that you do not use any trademarked terms in your company name.

Follow the prompts and enter the relevant information. You will need to have a registered agent (typically, that will be you). The registered agent is, in this case, the individual that accepts tax and legal documents on behalf of the business. The registered agent would also accept service of process if the business were ever sued.

You will also need to indicate the names of the members of the LLC. If you're like me, a one-person shop, you will have a single-member LLC, and that is perfectly okay.

What information do you need to set up your LLC?

The two main documents that you should file with your state's corporation commission when you establish your LLC are the Articles of Organization and the Operating Agreement. You generally upload these documents to your state corporation commission website when you establish your LLC. You should also keep digital and paper copies at your home or office. These documents are addressed below.

Articles of Organization

You will need to submit Articles of Organization for your LLC. Articles of Organization constitute a formal legal document that establishes the LLC with the state. The Articles set forth the rules for how that particular LLC operates. The Articles create the powers, rights, and duties of the LLC, and enumerate any other obligations between LLC members and between the LLC entity and its members.

You can certainly hire an attorney to draft the Articles for you. You can also search sites like legalzoom for a template specific to your state. You need to make sure that you include any state-required language in your Articles. Any required language will be set forth in your resident state's LLC Act.

The Articles of Organization must generally set forth the name of the company, the address of the principal office, and the name and address of the registered agent for service of process. In a single-member LLC, these addresses will typically be your home or permanent office. You must include a physical address, not a post office box. Note, however, that this address that you provide does not have to be the same as the mailing address you use for your LLC.

For your business' mailing address, it is strongly recommended that you use a post office box for privacy reasons. The mailing address of your publishing company will be included in the front matter of your book. There is no way I would make my home address available to the public.

In addition to the above, the Articles of Organization must generally include the name and address of each organizer or member (if you have additional members other than just yourself); whether the company is formed to exist only for a limited amount of time (this will likely not apply to you); and whether the LLC is member-managed or manager-managed (again, this is irrelevant if you are a single-member LLC). Any optional terms may also be included, as long as they are consistent with state law.

5

Operating Agreement

You will need to draft your LLC's Operating Agreement. The Operating Agreement governs how the LLC is managed, similar to bylaws for a corporation. The Operating Agreement typically sets forth in detail how business is conducted, the relationship of members to each other (if applicable), and voting rights of members (again, applicable if your LLC has multiple members).

Remember that no provision of your Operating Agreement can conflict with state law. Typically, any provision of your Operating Agreement that conflicts with state law would have no legal effect. For an example of state law governing LLC Operating Agreements, see Section 13.1-1023 of the Virginia Limited Liability Company Act. See also this article from the Small Business Administration on LLC Operating Agreements.

LLC Fees

The fees to set up and maintain your LLC are pretty low. At the time of this writing, in Virginia you pay $100 to initially establish the LLC. In addition, you pay $50 per year to maintain the LLC as an active corporate entity. Remember that you can declare these fees as business expenses on your income taxes.

Who makes the management decisions for an LLC?

Where a corporation has shareholders, an LLC has members. If you are the sole owner and member of the LLC, then you obviously make all the management decisions.

If you have an LLC with more than one member, then you need to select a management structure. An LLC can be member-managed or manager-managed. In a member-managed LLC, all the members together collectively manage and make decisions for the LLC. Each owner (member) is an agent of the LLC and can act on behalf of the LLC by, e.g., entering into contracts, borrowing money, and making other business decisions. Typically, the LLC members need to vote to approve these management decisions. Voting structure and voting rights are set forth in your Operating Agreement.

Member authority can also be limited in the Articles of Organization, if permitted by state law. Members may have an equal say in management, or authority can be proportional to the amount of money invested in the business. Alternatively, management authority can be structured in some other way. It is up to members to determine how much authority each member has. How the management is structured and how much say members have should be indicated in the LLC's Articles of Organization and the Operating Agreement.

In a manager-managed LLC, members select one manager to make decisions for the LLC.

If you do not indicate a management structure in your Articles of Organization, then, should any disputes arise, state law will impose a management structure by default. Typically, the default is the member-managed structure.

The corporation

Corporations are being used less frequently by small business owners, who largely favor using the LLC. Nevertheless, corporations are another limited-liability option for you.

Similar to the LLC, you set up your corporation with your state corporation commission. You will need to submit Articles of

Incorporation, the legal document that establishes the existence of your corporation. You will need to indicate the members of your corporation. You will also need to draft bylaws, which govern how the corporation is operated. The bylaws indicate the authority of members and how business is conducted.

Corporations are governed under state law. Each state has a specific law that governs the establishment and operation of corporations. For example, see the Virginia Stock Corporation Act.

At the time of this writing, the fee to establish a stock corporation in Virginia starts at $75, depending on the number of shares.[1] The annual registration fee for stock corporations is also based on the number of authorized shares.[2] The fee to establish a nonstock corporation in Virginia is $75[3] and the annual registration fee for a nonstock corporation in Virginia is only $25.[4] In Virginia, most nonstock corporations are created for non-profit or charitable purposes.

The biggest difference between the LLC and corporation deals with how owners need to respect the corporate form. The term "corporate form" refers to the technical requirements that business owners must fulfill in order to keep the entity's assets separate from personal assets. This separation is necessary in order for the business owner to get limited liability protection. Corporate form is addressed below.

Can a fictitious name or dba be used instead of establishing an LLC or corporation?

A fictitious name is a name that a person, including an individual or business entity, uses instead of the person's true name. Typically, the fictitious name, also called an "assumed name," "trade name," or "doing business as" ("dba"), is used in the course of transacting business.

You can certainly use a fictitious name for your author business, if that is your preference. However, use of a fictitious name as an individual, without setting up the limited liability corporate entities discussed above, does not grant you any of the limited liability protection. You can only get that limited liability protection by establishing a limited liability entity.

When to set up your limited liability company or corporation

The earlier, the better. Set it up right away, preferably before you publish your first book. You will likely need to fund your business account with personal income before you earn any royalties. That is fine and does not mean that you cannot get the limited liability protection discussed above. You can fund your business account minimally so that the company is set up by the time you publish your first book.

If you self-publish your first book under your own name as a sole proprietor, it's a hassle to republish under your newly created corporate entity later (but it is possible). For this reason, it is recommended that you set up your business entity before you publish anything.

How to make sure you get limited liability protection

In order to get the limited liability protection offered by an LLC or corporation, you must do more than merely establish the business entity. If you set up an LLC or corporation in name only and do not take the steps to respect the corporate form, then you run the risk of losing the limited liability protection.

If a Plaintiff sues an LLC or corporation, the Plaintiff can only potentially recover the assets of the LLC or corporation. If the company does not have a lot of assets or income, the Plaintiff may argue that the owner(s) of the company should be held liable, such that the Plaintiff could recover damages from the owner(s)' personal assets. This is the situation that you want to avoid. You should limit any potential liability you may have to your company's assets, so that your personal assets are not accessible.

To get the limited liability, you must respect the corporate form. Essentially, this means that you must take the necessary steps to maintain your personal assets and finances separate from business assets and finances. Further, you must follow certain corporate formalities and rules. If you fail to do this, there is a chance that a court will pierce the corporate veil, i.e., disregard the corporate form of the entity.

When a court disregards the corporate form of your business, your limited liability goes out the window and your personal assets and income may be recoverable should a Plaintiff prevail in a lawsuit against you. Courts may also disregard the corporate form and limited liability to prevent fraud and other injustices, which are discussed in more detail below.

In addition, if someone uses the business entity to further their own individual ends, that may also serve as a basis for a court to disregard the limited liability of an LLC or corporation. An LLC member (owner) must act with a common-law duty of care. That is, the LLC owner must act in the best interests of the LLC, not of the individual owner(s) of the LLC. In the case of a corporation with shareholders, the business owner must act in the best interests of shareholders.

How to respect corporate formalities

This section discusses how to respect the corporate form by maintaining your business separate from your personal life. In many states, the failure of an LLC to observe these corporate formalities alone is not sufficient ground for losing limited liability and imposing personal liability. You can check with a local attorney to be sure of the laws in your state.

The rules regarding corporations are stricter. If you opt to set up a corporation, failure to follow the rules below may cause you to lose the limited liability protection.

Whether you operate as an LLC or corporation, when you follow these formalities the chance that you may lose limited liability decreases. For these reasons, it is strongly recommended that you follow these guidelines.

Maintain a separate business checking account

Keep a separate business checking account, which holds only those funds related to your author business. Keep your personal checking and savings accounts separate. Now, it is typically fine to fund your business from your personal assets (almost everyone does when establishing a business). Partially funding your business from personal assets, such as from your day job salary, will not typically negate limited liability unless there are other factors.

Maintain a separate business email address

Set up a separate email address for business-related communication. Do not use your personal email address. This is another step which reflects that your business dealings are separate from your personal life.

Establish a post office box dedicated to your business to receive business mail

Your business address will typically appear in the front matter of your book, on the copyright page that lists the publishing company. It is highly recommended that you set up a post office box to use as your business mailing address, and that you do NOT list your home address. If you list your home address, then anyone looking at the copyright page of your book has access to it.

Use the appropriate business abbreviation

Whenever you use your business name, including in any publication, on business cards, and in correspondence, use the abbreviation for the business, e.g., Eighth House Press, LLC, or ABC Company, Inc. (for a corporation). Using the business abbreviation puts people on notice that they are dealing with a limited liability business. It's good business practice, and another method to show that your business assets are separate from your personal assets. Some states legally require you to use this abbreviation in your company's name. For example, the Virginia Limited Liability Company Act mandates:

A limited liability company name shall contain the words "limited company" or "limited liability company" or their abbreviations "L.C.," "LC," "L.L.C.," or "LLC."[5]

Get a business credit or debit card to use for business-related expenses

Again, the purpose of having a business credit card is to maintain business-related expenses and income separate from your personal expenses and income.

It is also easier to declare your author business expenses on your taxes if you maintain them clearly separate from your personal expenses.

In addition to the above recommendations, corporations typically have more technical rules that you need to meet in order to respect the corporate form and get the limited liability protection. Corporations have the ability to issue stock for their shareholders, who are part owners of the corporation. For this reason, corporations typically require more filings and fees to remain in compliance with state law.

Corporations also typically have stricter rules about record-keeping and holding regular meetings than an LLC For example, the S corporation, the corporation that is typically best for small businesses, can have up to 100 shareholders. The S corporation must hold and keep minutes of regular shareholder meetings. The LLC does not have this requirement. If you're a single-member LLC, like I am, there aren't really any big advantages to setting up an S corporation instead of an LLC.

A note on state corporate law versus federal tax law

This issue is often confused in online small business groups, so it is worth noting here.

Typically, LLCs, including single-member LLCs, get limited liability protection. This determination is based on state law, so make sure you research the law in your jurisdiction.

However, single-member LLCs report income under federal law the same way sole proprietorships do. This is a big advantage to the LLC form. The LLC offers pass-through taxation, where the LLC does not pay any LLC or corporate tax. Instead, the LLC's income and expenses pass through to the LLC owner's personal tax returns, and the owner pays personal income tax on the company's *profits* (or declares the company's losses as *their* losses). That is, you pay taxes on the profits from your author business, which equate to your revenue less business expenses. For this reason, it is essential to keep all records of expenses associated with your author business.

An S corporation may also get the pass-through taxation, but a C corporation (typically for bigger entities that plan to offer shares publicly at some point) is typically taxed twice, once at the corporate level and again on distributions to shareholders.

How entities report their income for federal tax purposes is a completely different issue than whether they are able to get limited liability under state corporate law if they are sued. Online commenters sometimes say things like, "Just do a fictitious name. It's not worth doing an LLC because single-member LLCs are treated the same as individuals." For federal tax law reporting purposes, yes, that is true. But establishing a single-member LLC still gets you the limited liability protection, which is extremely valuable to a small business owner. Please do not get any advice from people commenting online. There is so much BAD legal and business advice out there!

These steps are time-consuming and not without expense. However, it is easier to do this work on the front end than pay legal counsel if you are forced to litigate. Further, these business-related expenses are tax-deductible. Make sure you keep organized records and receipts.

What Plaintiffs could potentially get from you under limited liability

This section discusses what a Plaintiff could recover if the Plaintiff can only recover from your LLC's assets, under the limited liability of the LLC.

Generally, an LLC is only liable for members or managers' conduct if it is in the ordinary course of business of the LLC or with authority of the LLC.

A Plaintiff cannot prevail in a lawsuit for activity outside the scope of the LLC's business. For example, a Plaintiff could not recover my LLC's assets if they sue me for assault in civil court, unless the assault is somehow connected with my business.

When people sue your LLC, they sue for monetary loss or damages. The liability, or the total amount of money damages a Plaintiff could recover, is generally limited to the contributions of each LLC member/manager. If your LLC is a single-member LLC, then the Plaintiff can generally only recover your contributions to the LLC.

There are exceptions to this general rule. For example, if the LLC's Articles of Organization allow for personal liability and the LLC member consented to personal liability in writing, then a Plaintiff could potentially recover from the member's personal assets.

Remember that a Plaintiff has to show actual money damages, or loss, to bring a legal action against your LLC.

How you can lose limited liability protection

Even if you respect corporate formalities and separate business income and assets from your personal income and assets, under certain circumstances you may still lose limited liability protection. This section addresses those particular circumstances under which you could potentially lose that protection.

As mentioned above, failure to observe the corporate formalities alone is often not sufficient for you to lose limited liability. See, for example, the Minnesota law:

> The failure of a limited liability company to observe formalities relating exclusively to the management of its internal affairs is not a ground for imposing liability on the members, managers, or governors for the debts, obligations, or other liabilities of the company.[6]

However, failure to follow those corporate formalities may make it easier for a Plaintiff to prove the claims discussed in this section.

First, I don't want to spook you. Limited liability is the default state for LLCs. It is difficult for a Plaintiff to prove that personal assets should be recoverable when the Defendant is an LLC. A

Plaintiff that brings a lawsuit against an LLC owner has the burden of proof to show why a court should disregard the limited liability of the entity.

Second, while in most states single-member LLCs get the full limited liability protection that LLCs offer, it is generally easier for Plaintiffs to persuade a court to disregard limited liability if the LLC only has one member. It's not *easy*, just *easier*. This trend should encourage you to maintain detailed business records and make sure that you respect the corporate formalities discussed above, including maintaining separate bank accounts, email addresses, and mailing addresses.

Lastly, the legal arguments discussed here are not hard-and-fast rules. Remember that there is no one-size-fits-all answer to the question of what a Plaintiff must show for a court to ignore limited liability. Corporate law is governed by state law, and each state has its own rules. Further, these particular laws are generally based not on state statutes, but on legal precedent reached through the development of court cases. To know the precise laws in your state, you should consult with a local attorney.

Determining whether to ignore the limited liability of an LLC is always a fact-specific scenario, highly dependent on the particular facts of the case at issue.

Below are summarized the main ways through which Plaintiffs could argue for your personal liability.

Unity of interest

This argument entails proving that there is no real separation between the company and the company's owner. This concept has also been referred to as the alter ego test, especially regarding corporations. Generally, a Plaintiff would have to prove that the owner is operating the business as an extension of themselves rather than as a separate entity. This can be proven through a variety of means, including showing that the owner uses the business' money for their own personal purposes.

Fraud

If the LLC owner commits fraud, then a court may ignore the division between the LLC and the LLC owner, thereby ignoring the limited liability protection. Fraud can be a civil or criminal matter. Civil fraud, the type most relevant here, generally involves a false representation of a material fact with the intent to defraud. A good example of a business fraud case would be a claim that the business owner promised services that they knew they could not deliver.

The most important part here is that the Plaintiff must show that the Defendant intended to falsely represent the material fact. In a civil fraud case, the Plaintiff must also prove that they suffered actual damages (usually in the form of money) because of the Defendant's fraudulent misrepresentation. A criminal fraud case is brought by the state (instead of being filed by a civil Plaintiff), and carries a possible punishment of fine or jail time rather than money damages.

In some states, proving fraud alone is not sufficient to lead a court to disregard limited liability. In some states, the Plaintiff must show fraud *and* unity of interest. Alternatively, if the LLC was created as a sham, and with the sole purpose of committing fraud or to make it easier for the perpetrators to commit fraud, then proving that element alone may be sufficient for a court to disregard limited liability.

Failure to follow duty of care

Another major way through which you may lose the limited liability protection of your LLC is by treating the business as your personal cash cow, using business assets for your own personal interests rather than for business interests. In other words, the owner does not act with a duty of care.

Whether you operate as a single-member LLC or an LLC with multiple members/ managers, you must act with a duty of care. That is, you must act in the best interests of the business, not in your personal best interests. If, instead, you act in your personal interests over those of the company, then courts may ignore the separation between you and the business. This in turn may lead courts to ignore the limited liability of the LLC.

Now, you obviously are operating the business to support yourself and your family, and that is perfectly fine. When a business is brand new, most business owners choose to invest the profits back into the business. Of course, the intention is that you will earn enough from your author business to financially support yourself and your family. As your business arrives at that point, you may consider choosing a certain amount of profit to invest back into the business and pay for business expenses (e.g., editing, cover design, advertising, software licenses, computers, entry fees for book festivals, etc.). And you may consider paying yourself a salary as your business' sole employee. Make sure you keep records clearly indicating the amount of the salary you pay yourself.

The elements of the duty of care depend on the laws and legal precedent of the relevant state. For example, the Virginia Limited Liability Company Act expressly requires that businesses act with the duty of care:

"A manager shall discharge his or its duties as a manager in accordance with the manager's good faith business judgment of the best interests of the limited liability company."[7]

In order to interpret exactly what this means, you need to consult with local legal counsel, who would be able to explain the precedent regarding duty of care in your jurisdiction.

A good example of the violation of the duty of care is *Dodge v. Ford Motor Company*,[8] a case in which the Michigan Supreme Court held that Henry Ford was obligated to operate Ford Motor Company in the best interest of shareholders. Henry Ford had made a decision that he wanted to donate the profits of his company to charity, and that from then on, Ford Motor Company would operate as a charitable organization. In line with this charitable business plan, Henry Ford lowered prices for consumers and raised salaries for employees. Ford indicated that shareholder profits were not a concern for him. While this is an admirable goal, the Court found that Henry Ford had a duty of care toward his shareholders, by which he was obligated to maximize profits.

If someone like Henry Ford wants to donate to charity, they may establish a nonprofit to do so. However, a corporation is not a nonprofit, and has a duty to maximize profits for shareholders. Corporation owners have a great deal of leeway in determining *how* to do business and *how* to maximize profits pursuant to the common law business judgment rule. However, they have a duty of care to act in the best interest of stockholders.

Unjust cost

Generally, if the LLC has unpaid debts, then the debts can only be repaid from the assets of the LLC, not the personal assets of the LLC members or managers.

The inability of a business to pay creditors alone is generally not sufficient for a court to disregard limited liability. However, if there is fraud *and* inability to pay creditors; or unity of interest *and* inability to pay creditors, then a court may disregard limited liability, depending on the legal precedent in that jurisdiction.

Remember that to bring a civil action, the Plaintiff must show that they suffered harm in some way, typically in the form of money damages. A Plaintiff is not able to bring a civil case merely because they do not like the business owner or think that the business owner is acting in their own personal interests over those of the business. These court cases arise when a Plaintiff loses money.

For example, the Plaintiff may have provided services to the business and has not received payment. Or the Plaintiff relied on/purchased services from the business that were not provided, and the Plaintiff consequently lost money. The Plaintiff must show damages and must prove that the damages were caused by the LLC.

State laws differ on the application of the above tests. In some states, such as Virginia, courts are very reluctant to ignore the limited liability of an LLC, and the Plaintiff has an uphill battle.

For example, pursuant to legal precedent in Virginia, to determine whether to disregard the limited liability of an LLC, the Plaintiff can show either unity of interest between company and owners, *or* that the entity is merely a device or sham use to conceal wrongs, fraud, or crime. In addition to either of those two factors, the Plaintiff must *also* show that adhering to the separation of business and owner would lead to an injustice.[9]

Virginia courts have also indicated that limited liability may be disregarded if the inability of the LLC to satisfy its debts and obligations is a result of deliberate undercapitalization, in a situation where the LLC is unable to pay its costs of doing business because its owners have intentionally underfunded it or siphoned money from it. As mentioned above, courts have also indicated that this test does not apply when the entity cannot pay because of bad business decisions, mismanagement or unexpected liabilities.[10]

Further, it is generally easier to get courts to ignore the limited liability of a corporation than an LLC, partly because there is much lengthier and older legal precedent regarding corporations. Further, rules and formalities for corporations are much stricter than for LLCs. For these, as well as other reasons discussed above, the LLC is the most popular entity for small businesses in the United States today.

A note on employing your children

I'm going to include one point of interest here. In the United States, you are legally permitted to employ your children in your business. Further, you are able to invest the money they earn from work in an Individual Retirement Account (IRA). The IRA is a tax-advantaged vehicle, which minors can use for educational expenses or later for retirement. This is an excellent way to save in a tax-advantaged manner for your children, to include them in helping the family team, and to teach them how to run a business.

Depending on the age of the child and other factors, the income your child earns from your business may be subject to income tax and Social Security/Medicare withholding. See IRS publication 15 for detailed information. Make sure that you keep records of the type of work they perform, the dates they work, and the amount they are paid. Make sure you pay them using a W-2.

Assigning your children business-related tasks also empowers them and makes them feel important. They can do tasks such as print, make copies, scan, and other administrative duties. Older children can even help proofread and produce and edit video ads for you. Consider employing your children in your author business!

Conclusion

You have learned how to set up and operate your limited liability business. You have also learned what you need to do to respect the corporate rules and formalities to maintain your limited liability status.

Now you are ready to establish and operate your LLC for your author business. Remember to take the above steps to maintain your business accounts and addresses separate from personal accounts and addresses. Further, make sure that you keep records and receipts of all expenditures to deduct them on your taxes.

Action steps:

1. Establish a limited liability company to publish your books.
2. Include the name of your LLC as the publisher in your books.
3. Make sure that you respect the corporate form and follow the necessary steps outlined in this chapter to get the limited liability protection in your state.
4. Keep all business expenses to deduct them on your taxes.

Copyright

This chapter is divided into two main parts. The first part discusses how to best protect your copyright over the written work that you create. The second part discusses how to request permission to use copyrighted works from other creators in your own books.

Protect your copyright to your own work

You have spent time, energy, and resources to create written works. Make sure that you adequately protect your copyright over your works. The process to do so is fairly simple and straightforward. Read on to find out how.

Why you should register your works with the U.S. Copyright Office

This is a question posed frequently among online author groups based in the United States: Should I register the books I write with the U.S. Copyright Office? The answer is Yes.

The U.S. Copyright Office is part of the U.S. Patent and Trademark Office. Whenever you create a copyrightable work, such as a book, you automatically have a protectable copyright over the work that you create, without needing to do anything. That is, the creation of the work gives you a copyright over the work. You do not have to register with the U.S. Copyright Office to have or assert copyright over your written work.

However, there is a huge advantage to registering your copyrightable written works with the Copyright Office. The registration permits you to have the option of obtaining statutory damages if you bring a successful legal action against a Defendant who infringes your copyright. These statutory damages are not available if you do not register your works with the U.S. Copyright Office.

If you have a legal action against someone who is using your written works without your permission, you can bring a lawsuit for copyright infringement. There is a three-year statute of limitations on bringing a civil copyright infringement case.[11] Most courts interpret the three-year statute of limitations to mean that a Plaintiff has three years from the date of discovery by the copyright holder to bring a lawsuit. If the Defendant argues that the statute of limitations has run out, such that the Plaintiff is barred from filing the claim, then the Defendant has the burden to prove whether the Plaintiff knew or, with due diligence should have known, about the alleged infringement.

Copyright law falls under federal law. The chapter above discussed how corporate law is governed by state law in terms of your limited liability company. Here, federal law applies. Copyright holders must file lawsuits for copyright infringement in federal court under the federal Copyright Act. Copyright holders can sue to recover actual damages (your actual financial loss) or statutory damages (a set amount based on the Copyright Act and any other relevant law).

Having statutory damages available can be advantageous, especially for works that are not commercially successful or have not yet been released to the market. If you are a newer author, and your work has not yet been commercially successful, or if you have not yet released your work to the market, you may not be able to show a high amount of actual damages, i.e., actual financial loss due to the copyright infringement.

Further, it is expensive to hire an attorney and bring a copyright infringement suit in federal court. You may decide not to bring the suit at all because your legal expenses would be greater than the amount of damages you could actually recover.

However, if you have registered your work with the U.S. Copyright Office, then you could sue to claim statutory damages, regardless of how little money you have made selling your books. If you sue for copyright infringement of a work that is registered with the U.S. Copyright Office, statutory damages range from $750 to $30,000 *per work*. If you can prove that the infringement was intentional or willful, then damages can be up to $150,000 *per work*. That is a significant amount of money for a new author or an author whose work has not yet been commercially successful.

Statutory damage protection is effective when the U.S. Copyright Office registers your copyright

Copyright holders only get the protection of statutory damages when the U.S. Copyright Office actually registers the copyright. In May 2019, the United States Supreme Court resolved a circuit court split by confirming this requirement in *Fourth Estate Public Benefit Corp. v. Wall-Street.com*.[12] The Court determined that registration occurs, and a copyright claimant may thereby seek statutory damages in an infringement suit, when the Copyright Office registers a copyright, as opposed to when the claimant files for the registration.

Plaintiff Fourth Estate Public Benefit Corp. argued, unsuccessfully, that it could file suit for statutory damages as soon as it submitted its completed application for registration. The Supreme Court disagreed. Filing for the copyright alone is therefore not sufficient to seek statutory damages in an infringement action.

Copyright infringement of works by newer authors appears to be on the rise. To that end, it is highly recommended that you register each of your finished works with the U.S. Copyright Office.

How to register with the U.S. Copyright Office

It is easy to register with the Copyright Office and can be done entirely online. Go to copyright.gov and click the link to register your work. At the time of this writing, the fee to register one book by a single author is $45. See the fee schedule here.

You can hire a patent/trademark attorney who specializes in copyrights to register your works for you. However, it is something that you can do yourself, so there is no need to hire an attorney to do it for you unless you want to delegate that responsibility to free up your time.

Action Steps:

1. Register all your finished written works (even if not yet published) with the U.S. Copyright Office. Keep all related documentation, including email confirmation. Make sure you are copyrighting the finished work, not a draft.
2. Maintain receipts for these filing expenses, since you can deduct them on your tax return.

* * *

How to use copyright-protected material in your works

This section discusses how to request permission to use copyrighted material created by other people in your own books.

If you are going to use copyrighted material created by other people in your books, then you need to make sure that you have written permission to use the material. This section specifically talks about the use of quotations from other written work, including song lyrics.

When you can use written works without permission from the copyright holder

First, this section addresses the use of works for which you do NOT need to obtain permission. You can generally use book titles, television show titles, movie titles, and song titles in your written work without needing permission from the copyright holder. For example, you can write that your characters listened to the song Thunderstruck by AC/DC without being required to get permission to use the song title.

Public domain works

You also do not need permission to quote from works that are in the public domain.

How do you know whether a work is a public domain work? A work may be in the public domain if the copyright has expired. Copyright protection does not last forever. Pursuant to the federal Copyright Act, a copyright of a work created after January 1, 1978 lasts for the author's life plus an additional seventy years.[13] Once that period has expired, works are in the public domain and may be used without permission.

A work may also be in the public domain if the author has failed to renew their copyright over the work. For works originally copyrighted between January 1, 1950, and December 31, 1963, copyrights that were in their first 28-year term on January 1, 1978, still had to be renewed to be protected for the second term.[14] If a valid renewal registration was made at the proper time, the second term would last for 67 years. However, if renewal registration for these works was not made within the statutory time limits, a copyright originally secured between 1950 and 1963 expired on December 31 of its 28th year, and protection was lost permanently.[15]

Lastly, a work may be in the public domain if the author intentionally placed the work in the public domain. For example, the author may include a dedication in a book, indicating that the book is placed in the public domain. Only the copyright owner has the right to place a work in the public domain. To this end, if you are going to cite from a public domain work, make sure that the person placing the work in the public domain has the legal right to do so.

Fair use doctrine

The fair use doctrine is a legal doctrine that promotes freedom of expression by permitting the unlicensed use of copyright-protected works in certain circumstances.[16]

Section 107 of the Copyright Act sets forth the criteria for whether citation to a written work falls under the fair use doctrine:

> "The fair use of a copyrighted work, including such use by reproduction in copies or phonorecords or by any other means specified by that section, for purposes such as criticism, comment, news reporting, teaching (including multiple copies for classroom use), scholarship, or research, is not an infringement of copyright."[17]

In determining whether the use of a work in a particular case falls under fair use, the following factors must be considered:

1. The purpose and character of the use, including whether such use is of a commercial nature or is for nonprofit educational purposes;
2. The nature of the copyrighted work;
3. The amount and substantiality of the portion used in relation to the copyrighted work as a whole; and

4. The effect of the use upon the potential market for or value of the copyrighted work.[18]

Whether use of a work falls under the fair use doctrine and does not require written permission from the copyright holder is a fact-based inquiry subject to legal interpretation. Courts litigate legal disputes regarding this matter.

It is recommended that if you have any doubt as to whether you need permission to use copyrighted material, err on the side of caution and request written permission from the copyright holder. It is more advisable to obtain written permission and not need it than the opposite. The section below addresses how to request permission from copyright holders.

How to request permission to use copyrighted material from books

To use a quotation from another written work in your book, short story, or other work, you need to request permission from the copyright holder. The best way to do this is to contact the publisher, which is listed on the copyright page in the front matter of the book or other work. The publisher may be a company or an individual. Find a mailing address or email for the publisher, which is usually included on the book's copyright page. Next, send a written request.

In your written request, include the following information:

1. Explain that you are an author of a book or short story, etc. Name the title of the work.
2. Indicate the expected date of publication of the book.
3. Indicate where you expect to publish the book (e.g., North America, worldwide, etc.).

4. State that you seek permission to reproduce the following content from the other written work. State the exact content that you want to quote in your work.

5. Indicate how you expect to use the content in the book (e.g., as an epigraph at the beginning of the book, at the beginning of the chapter, within the text, etc.). Here, give as much context as possible. You will likely want to include the pages of your book where you quote the copyrightable content, so that the copyright holder can see the relevant context.

6. Include your full name and contact information.

7. If you have not received a reply in a couple of weeks, recontact to follow-up.

Typically, you will pay a fee to the copyright holder to use the content. The amount of the fee varies widely and is at the discretion of the copyright holder. If the copyright holder is a self-published author, perhaps there will be no fee.

How to request permission to use copyrighted material from song lyrics

To use song lyrics in your written work, you need to request written permission from the copyright holder, which is typically a music company or producer. Below, we go through this process step-by-step, which is slightly more complicated than requesting permission to use material from books.

Find the copyright holder of the particular song

To quote song lyrics, authors need to request permission from the music company that holds the rights to the song.

All music producers and songwriters must belong to one of these companies: www.ascap.com, www.bmi.com, or www.sesac.com.

Start by going to these websites and searching for the song in which you are interested. When you find the right song, the listing will include the name of the copyright holder.

To use my search as an example, I searched for the song *We Belong* (performed by Pat Benatar) on www.bmi.com. Here is the entry I got:

"Publisher" here denotes the copyright holder. When I clicked on the publisher's name, I got this info:

Next, draft a letter and email it to the email address listed (here, info@sonyatv.com). Screen Gems/EMI Publishing was acquired by Sony in 2012; therefore, the copyright holder is now SonyATV. Further, note the songwriter/composer names, which you will need to include in your permission letter.

Draft the permission letter

Email a letter requesting permission to the email address listed for the publisher/copyright holder. Alternatively, you can send a letter by postal mail, but emails typically get a faster response. The letter should explain the following:

1. Explain that you are an author of a book or other written work and name the work's title.
2. Indicate the expected date of publication of the book.
3. Indicate where you expect to publish the book (e.g., North America, worldwide, etc.).

4. State that you seek permission to reproduce the following lyrics from the song. Indicate the lyrics as well as the songwriters and performer.

5. Indicate how you expect to use the lyrics in the book (e.g., as an epigraph at the beginning of the book, at the beginning of the chapter, within the text, etc.). Here, give as much context as possible. You will likely want to include the pages of your book where you quote the lyrics, so that the copyright holder can see the relevant context.

Follow the company's specific procedures to request permission

Like in any big company, after you make your initial request you may get the runaround. You likely will be bounced around until you get to the right person and the right form.

After emailing my permission letter, I received an automatic reply indicating several email addresses for specific areas of inquiry:

Automatic reply: Request permission to use song lyrics   Inbox ×

Info@sonyatv.com via sony.onmicrosoft.com
to me ▾
Thu, Mar 14, 3:54 PM

Hello and thank you for contacting Sony/ATV Music Publishing. If you are contacting us for any of the reasons below, please use the corresponding email addresses and websites:

Sync License (Film, TV, Youtube, Games etc): filmTVinquiries@sonyatv.com
Live Stage License (Plays, Live Performances/Productions: livestageinquiries@sonyatv.com
Advertising License (Commercials, Video Ads): advertisinginquiries@sonyatv.com
Mechanical License (Album, Recording Project): www.harryfox.com
Sample License (Remixes, Music Snippets, Mashups) samplingus@sonyatv.com
Print License(Books, Sheet Music Copies): licensing@sonyatv.com
SCORE (Online Client Account): scoresupport.us@sonyatv.com
Change of Address changeofaddress@sonyatv.com
Royalties (Client checks, deposits and/or statements): royaltyquestions@sonyatv.com
Other info@sonyatv.com (if you fit this category, you do not have to resend your initial email)

I resent my permission letter to the Print License email address listed in the above email.

Next, I received an email from an actual person, indicating that I had to make the request using their online form:

Hi Maria

We have received your letter requesting a lyric reprint for the song "We Belong" (Lowen / Navarro). I have attached our reprint permission form, if you could fill it out and get it back to me that would be great. Let me know if you have any questions.

Thanks!

Licensing and Income Tracking Coordinator
Sony/ATV Music Publishing | 424 Church Street, Suite 1200 | Nashville, TN 37219
615 743 1954 (office)
megan.lanzotti@sonyatv.com | www.sonyatv.com

Sony/ATV
MUSIC PUBLISHING

I completed the record company's form, emailed it and received yet another email, requesting that I submit the company's online form specific to print license requests.

I completed and submitted the online form again. In response, I received an automatic message indicating that I could expect a reply in four to eight weeks' time.

After several weeks, I decided that I no longer wanted to delay publication of my book. I went ahead and published my book without using the song lyrics. Several months after publication, I received an email from someone at SonyATV asking me if I still wanted a written license to use the song lyrics. I declined, indicating that I had already published my book.

What if you don't hear back at all?

As long as you have evidence that you reasonably attempted to obtain permission, one option is that you go ahead and use the lyrics in your written work. If you decide to use the lyrics, you should indicate on the imprint page of your book language akin to, "all reasonable efforts were made to contact the copyright holders." And remember to keep all relevant paperwork and emails so that you can prove that you tried to request permission from the copyright holder.

The other option is not to use the lyrics at all. If it were me, and I did not receive written permission, I personally would not use the lyrics because I would not want the hassle of a possible lawsuit. An alternative would be to mention the title of the song (for which you do NOT need permission) instead of using the lyrics.

What happens if you use copyrighted material without permission

If you quote a book or song lyric in your written work and do not request permission, then you open yourself up to potential liability. The copyright holder has a legal basis to sue you.

The copyright holder may or may not decide to sue, depending on how much money the copyright holder has to litigate, and how much money *you* have as the Defendant. If the Defendant has little resources, then the copyright holder may decide not to bother with a lawsuit at all. Of course, since you have formed a limited liability company as discussed above, you have protected your personal assets and income from possible litigation.

The possibility that you may be sued is particularly acute if you use song lyrics without permission. If you quote song lyrics without a written license to do so, the music company or producer that holds the rights to the song has a legal claim against you. Music producers have a lot of money and resources, and most new self-published authors would be quickly outspent in a lawsuit against them. You could hire an attorney and argue fair use in federal court, but that would cost you a ton of money. The only winners in that scenario are the attorneys, at your expense.

If you are risk-averse, like me, you will likely want to go ahead and request permission to use the song lyrics, without having to fall back to litigating the issue of fair use.

Conclusion

Now you know the most important information about protecting your copyright over your written work, as well as how to request written permission to use others' copyrighted material.

While time-consuming, these steps are not difficult and can be accomplished almost entirely online.

Action Steps

1. If you want to use book excerpts, song lyrics, or other written copyrighted material in your own written work, make sure you request written permission for such use.
2. Start the process to request permission as soon as possible, well in advance of publication, since it can take a long time. Otherwise, you risk delaying publication.
3. Maintain all receipts of expenditures to deduct them on your tax return.

Defamation

This chapter discusses how to best protect yourself from any potential defamation claims. The following question is often asked in author forums: Can I write about this particular person without legal consequences? I even talked to one author who told me that an acquaintance of his wanted him to use the acquaintance as a character in his novel.

Of course, since you have set up your limited liability company as discussed above, you have protected your personal assets and income from any potential litigation. Still, none of us want to deal with a lawsuit, even if we are in the right.

This chapter first addresses what defamation means, then discusses how to protect yourself from potential defamation litigation.

This chapter addresses libel, or written defamation, since it addresses defamation claims associated with your written works. Oral defamation is known as slander.

There is no surefire way to fully protect yourself from defamation claims, especially if you write nonfiction. Further, remember that anyone can bring a lawsuit. Whether the lawsuit actually has merit, or whether the Plaintiff has set forth all the relevant elements of the claim, is another question. Just because someone has brought a lawsuit against you does not mean that they are able to prove all the elements of that claim. In the United States, it is easy to bring a lawsuit, many of which are frivolous.

Even if you win a case, you still need to spend money litigating the case in state court, which can easily turn into a five-figure sum. You want to be able to nip any potential litigation in the bud. To this end, there are steps you can take in order to decrease litigation risk.

Proving the elements of defamation claims

Defamation is a matter governed by state law, just like the corporate laws pertaining to your limited liability company. You can consult with a local attorney to know the specific elements a Plaintiff would need to prove in order to successfully bring a defamation lawsuit in your state.

In order to win a defamation case, a Plaintiff needs to show that all the elements of defamation have been met. Since defamation is governed by state law, the elements necessary to prove defamation differ on a state-specific basis. However, they will generally be similar to the following.

There must be an actionable statement

First, there must be an actionable statement that concerns the Plaintiff. Such a statement must be published via oral or written means (here, publication in your written works). "Actionable" means that the statement must be false *and* defamatory.

Second, the publisher of the defamatory statement must have the requisite intent to harm the reputation of the Plaintiff. It is generally not necessary for the Plaintiff to show that the Defendant *knew* that the statement was false. It is enough to show that the Defendant acted recklessly or negligently in failing to verify the truth of the statement.

Third, generally the Plaintiff needs to prove economic harm (monetary damages) to win a defamation case, usually by showing loss of income. However, in some states this element is not necessary. In some states, it is enough for the Plaintiff to prove "pain and suffering," usually in the form of emotional distress or mental anguish. In the latter cases, the damage is considered to be the harm to the Plaintiff's reputation.

What does "defamatory" mean?

What makes a statement "defamatory?" First, just because a statement is false does not necessarily mean that it is defamatory. False statements alone are not actionable defamatory statements.

Second, the definition of defamatory depends on state law, but will be close to the manner in which the state of Virginia defines it:

> "All words shall be actionable which from their usual construction and common acceptance are construed as insults and tend to violence and breach of the peace."[19]

Insults and words that deal with violence or provoke violence and breach of the peace are therefore considered defamatory in Virginia. What this means exactly is a matter of legal interpretation and case precedent. For example, purposely lying about someone's age may or may not be an insult, depending on the statement and context. Further, opinions generally cannot be defamatory statements because they are not statements of fact.

Certain categories of statements are presumed to be defamatory. If the Plaintiff shows that the statement falls under one of these categories, then the statement is presumed to be defamatory and there is usually no need to litigate that particular matter:

1. Statements that indicate that the person committed a criminal offense involving moral turpitude. "Moral turpitude" is subject to legal interpretation based on case law, but generally means a crime that is done recklessly or with evil intent, and which shocks the public conscience as inherently base, vile, or depraved.

2. Statements that indicate that a person is infected with a contagious disease, where if the charge is true, it would exclude the person from society.

3. Statements which impute to a person unfitness to perform the duties of an office or employment, or lack of integrity in the discharge of the duties of such an office or employment.

4. Statements which prejudice the person in their profession or trade.

With respect to statements in the above categories, the court will presume that the Plaintiff's reputation has been damaged as a result, thereby making it easier for the Plaintiff to succeed on the merits of the defamation case.

Generally, statements that fall outside of these categories are subject to legal interpretation and case precedent as to whether or not they are defamatory.

There is a much higher standard of proof involved to prove defamation against a public figure. The term "public figure" includes a famous person, not necessarily someone who holds public office. To prove that a Defendant made a defamatory statement against a public figure, the Plaintiff must show that the Defendant acted with actual malice under a standard of clear and convincing evidence (generally a higher standard than in most civil claims). "Actual malice" means that the Defendant either knew the statement was false or acted with reckless disregard as to whether or not it was true.

Steps to take to protect yourself from defamation litigation

This section discusses the specific steps you can take to protect yourself as much as possible from potential defamation litigation.

Nonfiction works

Defamation usually comes up in the context of nonfiction works, since you are writing about real people and real events. If you are writing a nonfiction account of events that actually happened, you can make sure that the facts you write about are completely accurate. The truth is an absolute defense to libel. If you are sued for defamation and can show, preferably through written evidence, that you made truthful statements about someone, the Plaintiff in a defamation lawsuit will not succeed. However, even if you write the actual truth, a Plaintiff could still bring a defamation case. And you may be stuck litigating the matter of truth, which can end up being very expensive.

A less riskier option would be to obscure the truth, so that characters are not individually identifiable by the reader.

If you are writing a fiction novel inspired by or based on real events, not an actual account of events, then you can obscure facts and not write the actual truth. In that case, it is recommended to include a disclaimer in the front matter, indicating that the events and characters are fiction. You could also indicate that the events are inspired by or based on real events, and that you have used creative liberty to change details. In this manner, you make clear that you are not representing what actually happened.

Further, if you, for example, are a medical professional discussing your patient cases in a book, make sure that you completely obscure the patient's identity. It is generally acceptable to write about a patient or client that suffered from such-and-such illness without noting any of the patient's particular attributes.

Obscuring character attributes becomes difficult when writing biographical works, especially those written in first person. Obviously, if an author writes a first-person autobiographical work and talks about their mother and father, the reader knows that the author is talking about their own parents. One would hope that the author's parents would not sue them for libel. However, I have seen stranger things happen. Do not assume anything.

As noted above, even if the author writes only about things that are true (truth being a defense to libel), an author could potentially spend tens or even hundreds of thousands of dollars litigating the matter of truth in a defamation lawsuit. Trust me, you do not want to find yourself in a knock-down, drag-out lawsuit.

One way to get around this potential pitfall is to write a creative nonfiction work, as opposed to a biography or autobiography, where the author writes in third person about, e.g., the main character's parents. By changing the main character's personality and appearance, as well as the setting of the story and other elements, a Plaintiff would have a much more difficult time proving that they are in fact the individual being discussed in the book.

Fiction works

Similar strategies apply to fiction works. Authors often write about characters inspired by real people. Again, you want to make sure that you do not write characters that are so specific that readers know that they could only be one single person. Authors should use different character attributes to mask that they are writing about a specific person. For example, you can change the gender, hair or eye color, and/or nationality of the character as compared to the actual person.

Include a disclaimer when appropriate

It is also good practice to include a disclaimer in your fiction or creative nonfiction work that all characters in this work are fictional and not based on any real people. Most authors incorporate bits and pieces of the personality and appearance of people they know personally in their work. However, discussing a particular individual is much different from discussing an individual who happens to have one characteristic of a real-life individual. In the latter case, you cannot really prove whom the author is talking about.

Should you request permission from nonfiction subjects?

This question is posed frequently. I lean towards No. If you are writing a nonfiction book and ask the subject for their permission to write about them, you are essentially admitting that you are writing about that individual. Even if they give you permission, they can still sue you for libel later and you may end up litigating the matter of truth. The fact that they gave you permission, oral or written, to write about them does not preclude them from suing you for defamation.

My recommendation here is therefore not to ask subjects for permission. My recommendation is to obscure details so that it is not clear that you are writing about that particular individual.

Conclusion

Defamation litigation is a real risk that authors face, but you can significantly lower your litigation risk by following the steps discussed above. To avoid potential defamation litigation, you should obscure facts and details so that characters are not so specifically drawn that they could only be one single individual.

Action Steps

1. If you write nonfiction works, to reduce litigation risk regarding a potential defamation claim, make sure that you obscure details about individuals so that they are not individually identifiable by the reader.
2. If you write fiction works and write about characters inspired by real people, make sure that you obscure details about individuals so that they are not individually identifiable by the reader.
3. Be very careful about admitting that any characters represent real people.

Conclusion

You are now equipped with the basic legal knowledge necessary to successfully operate your author business. While this guide is certainly not exhaustive, the information presented here is a good start to legally protecting your author business and limiting your potential liability as you grow your business.

Once you start thinking in terms of limiting your liability, it becomes second nature, and you will naturally take the steps to do so.

If you have any questions, please email me on maria@lawschool-heretic.com and I will try my best to assist.

Thank you for reading.

THE END

It would be greatly appreciated if you could leave an honest review of this book on Amazon and Goodreads. Thank you!

Notes

LIMITED LIABILITY PROTECTION

1   https://www.scc.virginia.gov/pages/Virginia-Stock-Corporations.

2   https://www.scc.virginia.gov/pages/Annual-Registration-Fees.

3   https://scc.virginia.gov/pages/Virginia-Nonstock-Corporations.

4   https://scc.virginia.gov/pages/Annual-Registration-Fees.

5   Virginia Limited Liability Company Act, § 13.1 - 1012(A).

6   Minnesota statute § 322C.0304(2).

7   Virginia Limited Liability Company Act, § 13.1-1024.1(A).

8   204 Mich. 459 (Mich. 1919).

9   *A.G. Dillard, Inc. v. Stonehaus Constr., LLC*, No. 151182, 2016 BL 178651 (Va. June 2, 2016).

10 *Dana v. 313 Freemason, A Condo. Ass'n*, 266 Va. 491 (Va. 2003).

COPYRIGHT

11 17 U.S.C. §507(b). Plaintiffs have five years to bring criminal infringement actions pursuant to 17 U.S.C. §507(a).

12 139 S. Ct. 881 (2019).

13 17 U.S. Code § 302(a). *See* https://www.copyright.gov/circs/circ15a.pdf.

14 https://www.copyright.gov/circs/circ15a.pdf.

15 *Id.*

16 https://www.copyright.gov/fair-use/more-info.html.

17 17 U.S. Code § 107.

18 *Id.*

DEFAMATION

19 Virginia Code Article 4 § 8.01-45.

About the Author

Maria Riegger is based in the Washington, DC area. She is a banking/corporate attorney by day (but please don't hold that against her), and an author by night.

Maria is a Gemini whose head has always been in the clouds. When she was bored as a child, she would make up stories in her head. She has been writing since she was about thirteen years old.

She has been caught air-guitaring in public. She loves to laugh, and is the "go-to" person if a friend needs someone to laugh at their lame jokes. In true Gemini fashion, she indulges both her logical personality as an attorney as well as her creative writing personality. She loved law school and even misses it, which has led her friends to conclude that she is certifiable. An irreverent Gen X'er, she writes irreverent fiction and nonfiction, with plenty of sarcasm.

You can connect with me on:

- http://www.lawschoolheretic.com
- http://twitter.com/RieggerM
- https://www.facebook.com/lawschoolheretic

Subscribe to my newsletter:

- http://eepurl.com/dAz9HH

Also by Maria R. Riegger

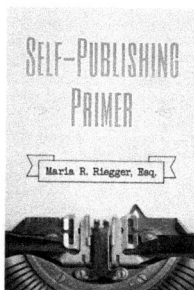

Self-Publishing Primer
Want help getting self-published?

Get your Self-Publishing Primer at https://l awschoolheretic.com/free-stuff/ for FREE.

I'm a self-published author who's been in the trenches. Let me help you. You'll get all the relevant info in one spot! I learned how to self-publish on the fly, and I'd like to let you in on what I know so that it's easier for you. This book is designed for the busy professional. Get all the essential information HERE.

Questions? maria@lawschoolheretic.com

Visit www.lawschoolheretic.com

Get your Self-Publishing Primer at https://lawschoolheretic.co m/free-stuff/ for FREE.

www.ingramcontent.com/pod-product-compliance
Lightning Source LLC
Chambersburg PA
CBHW071443210326
41597CB00020B/3920